the field

robert andrew perez

the field

omnidawn publishing
oakland, california
2016

Cover art © Job Piston, *David*

Cover and interior text set in Highway Gothic and Gill Sans Std

Cover and interior design by Gillian Olivia Blythe Hamel

Offset printed in the United States
by Edwards Brothers Malloy, Ann Arbor, Michigan
On 55# Glatfelter B18 Antique
Acid Free Archival Quality Recycled Paper

Library of Congress Cataloging-in-Publication data

Names: Perez, Robert Andrew, 1984- author.
Title: The field / Robert Andrew Perez.
Description: Oakland, California : Omnidawn Publishing, 2016. | "This is the author's first collection of poetry" -- Publisher's comment.
Identifiers: LCCN 2016014887 | ISBN 9781632430298 (pbk. : alk. paper)
Classification: LCC PS3616.E7436 A6 2016 | DDC 811/.6--dc23
LC record available at https://lccn.loc.gov/2016014887

Published by Omnidawn Publishing, Oakland, California
www.omnidawn.com (510) 237-5472 (800) 792-4957
10 9 8 7 6 5 4 3 2 1
ISBN: 978-1-63243-029-8

I can't think of many contemporary poets who have so inventively taken up the tools Jack Spicer left lying around for us, but in *the field* Robert Andrew Perez reminds us that poems can be games, can be riddles; that a book of poetry can read like a book of activities ("fill this box with stars"). But these poems are after the Beatles, after disco, after hip-hop and after grunge, after reality TV, after feminism, after psychedelia, after queer theory, after #YOLO, after AIDS. They are more Ovidian than Spicer was—"the void dissembles increments of blue / at itself"—and more trippy. They are deeply Californian poems, but you can take them with you anywhere: they are built to travel, sturdy and light. They let you watch them dancing in the bedroom and napping on the beach. They're both volatile and steady at the wheel: how does he do that? They are curious and fearless: "*What is dark matter* // What does dark matter?"

—*Chris Nealon*

contents

erasure	13
hypnagogia logia	15
a child i don't know asks me what tragedy is	16
hypnagogia logia	22
adult contemporary	23
hypnagogia logia	25
this world	26
hailing clouds	28
asperatus	30
hypnagogia logia	31
never been kissed	32
winter poem	34
enantiodromia	36
story of color	38
geminids	39

a desert sonnet 40

forest of mirrors 41

hypnagogia logia 46

santa cruz, ca 47

weekend 48

late summer 49

love poem 51

hypnagogia logia 52

poppies. poppies. 53

...until you have gone there,
and gone there, "into the

field," vowing Only until
there's nothing more
I want—

—Carl Phillips

erasure

my friends are writing poems for/about their kids, and here i am
still writing about fucking guys and fucking losing guys and fucking
loser guys and fucking loose guys, fucking losing loose, loser
guys. i do write about milk, but not breast milk. i'm more like

that dancing milk carton from the *coffee and tv* music video—at the end
i float to heaven with a strawberry milk carton, underscored by organ
music, except it's hell. pre-fire, that is to say before the kiln, the shape
of the vase fully formed. formed fully and undone, my state, figuratively,

is pre-fire. i carry the threat of combustion; all i need is sapphire.
let's think back to seeing nicole richie in a papasan in the westwood
urban outfitters. she corroborates my impulse to buy a blue jacket
i'll never wear, but in that moment i feel the burn of stardom. no one

knows me or nicole anymore. the preeminent callipygian, kim kardashian,
smatters minstrelsy on paper. destiny's progeny has a name for this:
jelly. we eat pulverized bone. purple is a flavor and grape is never
funny. with everything falling apart, why can't the monolith of patriarchy?

just because i care, i can never write a good poem for womyn. i watch
shonda rimes because i care about race and gender. because i love soap.
to drop it. before i knew erasure did it first, i assumed wheatus wrote
the lines: *i try to discover a little something to make me sweeter.*

oh baby refrain from breaking my heart. anything successfully invisible is also indelible. therefore i love him not. something partly loved, then, is able to be smeared and eventually wiped clean away. the children i never have and the poems i never write, therefore, i fully love them.

hypnagogia logia

there are many hes: a he of the past past, the recent past, of the now, a he of the he of the past past & the now, a he comprised in any assortment of the previously mentioned. which he of the phantasmagorical real did the many hes of the dream represent if any? were all the hes just a singular he veiled in clear confusion?

the he pressed his lips against the sleeper. neither brought the other out of the scene, out of [ ] why else, then, the lack of scent? why else would it be any he of the certain hes?

a child i don't know asks me what tragedy is

my initial impulse is to say, a goat song, but i don't feel
like explaining to him what the festivals of dionysus were—or
couldn't remember (dionysia amnesia)—so i tell him
several love stories, the same ones told to me when i asked:

i

he said, meet me here. she said, meet me here
instead. they agreed & both were late

to the wrong place. they tried again then later
fell in love. while in love, he said, i love you

for the first time *in his life*. she said, i love you
back. more time passed & they fell out of love

but continued to say the words. one day,
when in the season of dying, she said, meet me

here. when he arrived, they saw each other
in a wash of grey light. it was cloudy. as he

moved closer to her, into focus, she began to feel
the words in her mouth like fire. i should have

left you so long ago, she finally said out loud.
you are the only woman i have ever loved.

ii

fill this box with stars:

(ten minutes later)

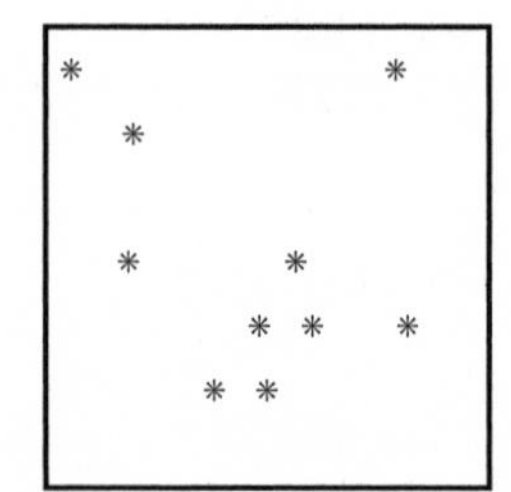

now think of the saddest thing you can think of.

now think of the happiest.

how many stars are missing from each box?

iii

let me answer your question with a question
whose voice do you hear when you imagine the plant saying water me*?*

iv

my last shot
to get you

to know
tragedy so

i act out
3 hours

of hamlet. you
remark everyone

is dead
i say ophelia

ophelia, ophelia
soaking wet

hypnagogia logia

this time it's a pizza on fire. i was trying to reheat it, and cook alongside four eggs. break shells. start flame. char cookie sheet. *what does* this *one mean?* she says nothing. i take it to mean it represents "nothing," that which ~~cripples~~ haunts my thinking. the yellow yolk goo slowly oozes to the edge of the ruined year. perhaps, in the fire, something hatched—a plan. an escape.

adult contemporary

at the present moment, the adjacency of the other city hums. we call that place just as home as the other, erasing/multiplying location; relocating the idea of home outside of geography. while we're at it, let's relocate sex, gender, race and the rest of what acts upon the tangible oozy soul box.

under the hum is an internalized beat (andante) alla dante, undulating. of the concentric rings we've looped, we choose the seventh to make our tent on. (a former version of us would've said *upon which to pitch our tent.*) we used to, like others, say home is temporary, but we always meant packable. tucked into a portmanteau, beneath the leaves & leaves of ramble, is the last home, origami'd neatly. a rectangle.

the trick i have yet to master is not ripping it when erecting it. like anything flat-packed, i give it a swedish name.

we had assigned songs to our epochs to trace time as melody. now that we've abandoned that for maps, time traces itself, without us.

there, in that body of water, that's my inner-deadbeat-father. those cascading hills, my inner-child. mum's the word. just a hum and some drumming. no more a young, skinny american idol. even the judges have moved on.

hypnagogia logia

it is [ ] appearance. there's a photo of him leaping through the air, as if taken just prior the sky being kicked open. there is another just like it of the other. this is a memory recurring, continually distorted. the dreamspeak speaks: don't remember so hard. the next time the sky may shatter & all the broken glass that doesn't fall in falls out. you may very well land on it.

this world

mid nights, we yield
to the meow of the web
& say *more* more

truism subs in
for truth, insofar that good
enough is good enough

for now. poetry is
an ultimate steganography
so the steganographer

hides his horcrux in lyric.
to vote, like prayer
is to believe in something

that will fail you. meet
a man about a verb.
met him? he's forgotten

about you, so as the world
turns, you become as necessary
as the word *reliquary*

but no more publishable
than a poem with the word
reliquary in it.

hailing clouds

a cumulus resembles
semen ribboning in chlorine

blue gene
pool of words:

ore comes from *ear*
or *earth* & *or-*

ifice comes from *mouth*
or *wound*

i am bound
to attach import
to a leftover ache
that is a beck

& call: you
there—the gondolier—
the lovelier

of us—with exposed opening

& closing heart valves—
imperfect halves
an exceptional hard-on-

yourself look
say: *blood clot-*

shaped cloud-ridden sky—screw
your moonlessness
& *your moonlessnessness*

then name it—

cirrus priapus
cirrocumulus thrombosis—

ad ripa—to reach
the shore
to arrive

asperatus

in 2009 the founder of the cloud appreciation society
along with his fellow arbiters announced a new formation

the sky has inverted earth's rolling hills siphoning the green
from them to make a blanket that waves

at god-time. *undulatus asperatus.* this is another/different
cloud poem. an ode, to our unmade bed, a gas-rendered

ceiling. pre-boiling-point forms impress each other
shifting the moistening cotton and foam. everything white

everything upside down. there is no distance in this metaphor
greater than its exactness. not likeness, equipoise.

the city we live in is known for steepness and sparseness
of anything flat. the soft, pliable earth is manipulated

by geothermal phenomena—hot giant invisible hands mold it.
our molten bodies. what we unmake shape heaven and earth.

hypnagogia logia

they were walking, the two, up the sidewalk each carrying a box of things. the boxes were of no importance. the trees they strolled beneath & the shadows that passed over them were of no importance either. not the way they swept across their faces as they sauntered along. (the boxes were light.) nor were the glances they eye stole of any importance. all that mattered, the dust mattering the windless air, was they walked their walk in complete hush.

never been kissed

i'm sitting next to a new boy who claims to not watch television, who prefers to read, but here we are watching *never been kissed.*

i associate one of my sexual awakenings with michael vartan. my on-and-off relationship to being an english teacher with him, too, and also cellar-door drew barrymore.

only watching this now can i see how wildly inappropriate their flirting is on that ferris wheel of love. they move through the tabooness of it the way bodies wade through water in a shallow pool. us sitting here, this is inappropriate, too.

mutual departure feels the same as being left. i guess the fact that this time i choose the pain marks maturity. no, i haven't forgotten to grieve but the momentum of newness pulls us forward.

as we've established, this couch is no ferris wheel of love & the ferris wheel of love is no ferris wheel of love. however, we can agree that we experience moving in a circle as moving forward, at least.

winter poem

you come to a wood peopled with trees
from the white noise of place forested
with men. your naked cells turn

the world's junk into heat—
debris to energy. a shivered brittle
timbre from the hoarfrost-crusted pines

underscore the otherwise dinless crowd
of deadwood. the gloam darkens gradually
like the word recessing further back

behind you, until the word is too far off
to distinguish from other twinkling specks
you see the plane of lake like linoleum

polluted with glitter & beer. the vacuum
inside you breaks—you can finally
hear the lubdub without the interfering music

of rumination. this rhythm of the night
is the snow that's like rain. you remove
a glove to trace the word onto cold glass

your heat clears the ice before you touch it
the solitude you once found retractable thins
you are who you no longer have beside you

enantiodromia

the notion that the laws of reality
cannot be changed
is an assumption.

atoms are made up
of leptons. eves, too.

that which hides
in the higgs bosom.

none of us is telling the truth.

night sky, in its mostly darkness,
is the most banal of mysteries.

who stands in the middle of the field?
a better science.

no one pulls out here.
we champion the ignorant light.
measure in lumens human densities.

tell me—
are you with me?

it's the conversion of something
into its opposite

that troubles us.
maybe there's enough thunder.

it is the only way to move.

story of color

according to the ways in which a child's brain is believed to work, color is an invention. if, say, the child had seen more photographs, he or she would believe the same about smiles. fiction is the preferred way of telling an accurate truth. the child's brain self-destructs & all that's left is an adult one. when the child claims to have seen a ghost, the adult does not necessarily lie in his or her denial of the event; he or she is merely sure of his or her sanity. the sane child, in his or her confusion, unable to reconcile what is believed to have been witnessed with what he or she is told, says, *but i am the ghost.* hugging the thin air, the adult says, of course you are.

geminids

for Carina

where we're in our hurtling we can see glitter
pouring out the black guts of our effigies

each multi-mile speck exhausting dust
light white skids unseeable to us

these ancestors of ice of rain can't crack
but sublimate my sister

how can one be reassuring when the nearly
nothing of us is comprised of nearly nothing

the thing that comprises everything
—it's never too late to start over

the brilliance of galactic scales
up the stem of speculation   *what is dark matter?*

what does dark matter? everything
is recoverable

when you discover everything is cover
chasms in chiasmus kiss this christmas

they the lights in a tree in a sky
moving not moving and moved

a desert sonnet

he supposes he would move "evan and hurf"
for her, he says over his breakfast serial

i listen to this flying over the expanse of track housing
the cashew and kidney pools

like turquoise healing stones

over the dirty chakras of sin city. vegas baby, like santa
baby, is flirtatious

in an obvious way. we know little of redemption and less of black jack.
i intend my funeral to be a black-tie affair—

coattail optional, open bar. from above condor height (out
of breadth)

i hear, why would i lie? the murky fog of truth is also a nakedness. the mind
is a cloud: write before it disappears.

ice is what makes it dark. what makes it thunder

forest of mirrors

to get to you i have to take steps
thru panes of glass
fuzzy site until a clearing
hi-def kills the ego
everything is a little bit different

each time

to get to you you have to hold
hands radiate the rocks & trees
purple-brown bars pulsate
language leaves, leaves language
everyone is mad
then everyone is happy
you pull me to each time

everything is a little bit different

when the i dies it resurrects itself
as eye questions living
the tree like history doesn't matter
only you are there, amnesia
a drama of croissantwich & banana
when the acid in the veins begins to wane
you come to a corporeal reality
not enough

to escape

the mirrored forest we walk again
everyone maddened
acid reflux vision quenched
i hold your hand down the hill
the camry is familiar but farther
everyone has always been family
the wobble of the world stabilizes
as you pull me out
you hold

madness over the mountain

tell me what you're thinking & feeling
answer with sickness
you need the crazy
brain know not to say love
recursive is the mind whatever
same inputs regurgitate the same
echo of discovering

the mirror is illusion

the drugs wane in waves
that is always returning
everything is a little bit different
i keep coming to
in a world no longer artificially
in flux a world not of fractals

but of matter
thought fugues
your hand no longer

pulling me through the forest of mirrors

the eyes bring you back
to the camera that was once outside you
blue sky over the blue granite
the void dissembles increments of blue
at itself the eye aligns the mind again
through you thought burrows through
the scrim of near-invisible barriers
to sanity down the sides the way
the hands of time blacken

it won't last forever

pray for & fear the euphonious joy
the world reassembles differently
before the trap of déjà vu only
you say we'll be on the balcony soon
food moves through the body
bodies move down the mountain
a new you for euphoria before thought-fugues
you no longer

pull me through the mirrored forest

love like light
is what is pulled

through glass
scatters

what reassembles dissembles the void
is only possible by you
it happens again differently
the metaphor of lifetime
scribbles the irrelevance of it
on madness mountain
where consciousness the lack of it
hovers, it won't last forever

will it? take my hand to pull
me out of time's glass
the watch reads 230 until it reads

521

acid wane: the wash of visuals
persist after the shower
nap to wake
to walk under the once swirling

moon & stars

are half-hidden like your waking dream
by the scrim of light blue night clouds
white against the void-black sky
not as if film

it is exactly like that, & the camera

unobscured—third eye—the camry
always farthering the road off the mountain
the forest mirrors
itself across the valley
some among them are killers
an echo

we sequester ourselves in a room

to let the field into us, despite
entropic bass violates, isolates
the forgiving pupil finally contracts
a fixity or fixation
each discrete ear harbors the same

secret universe, the field expands

hypnagogia logia

the smoke came as a surprise, seeping out of some device. the heat was secondary and it happened secondarily. was it the hood of a car? ~~a vacuum?~~ a laptop computer keyboard? it could have been any number of quotidian things that had crevices through which smoke could spill. any object that could take a while to get hot-to-the-touch.

someone who felt like me felt like a ~~cartoon~~ wolf. then something like a crotch came down the stairs, venus rising from sea-foam and wet genitals walking to shore. plumes of white steam, right then, blew out of all ears.

santa cruz, ca

a system moves over the strand
i see it, & though not a digital capture,
recorded—a panorama

moreover, i feel it as wind moving past
an inconsequential wall   slowed whistle

through thistle   i hadn't yet held your hand
unenthused by polygonal spirits

till we walked barefoot in the not-dream
to the edge of east cliff   cold ocean under
the arches, undertow   the arches

each of us is our own tree   palms refusing light
between them
the peril of a first is the threat of onlyness

due north, due south duet:
two weathervanes on one roof

weekend

choose a window upon which to
assign a narrative that thus
decides whether

we wear pants or shorts. floral
or a solid earth-

tone like blood-orange
nantucket red   people salmon
their way up through the panhandle

we cook our kale with onions
& yellow beets to beats by deptford goth

bay to breakfast. braid our hands

like challah. this morning began the end
of the weekend which begins the week

until the next i see you   pull up
the future is far away, let's repeat it

late summer

the sea or bay—
actually—is

enough. a handful
fits in the mouth
easy. gone is gone

is gone. in poetry school
& in life you learn a word

is elegy
for that which it signifies (a rule
of semantics) by way

of stevens. by way of the sea.
how dry. even this *sea*: dry.
a house neatly
built

of popsicle sticks.
an herb garden

resting

on a ledge above
the sink.
steam filtering through basil

leaves. hot water & porcelain.
by this logic, *elegy* is an elegy of an elegy.
and grief a failure

of necromancy.
zombie poem, be.

love poem

i saw your beard before me growing
then—around you—the trees & lichen

i took my drug money to use
on sandwiches for us

two hours i sat with the sun beating my face
that was smiling

every time i come up for air is the time i remember
i was drowning when you remind me

without saying & you are the air

hypnagogia logia

in the beginning she knew nothing more than the i did, then the i shattered into her, dissolving into blankness, a white-wash of pure [ ] she was a string taut beyond vibration.

in the negative space of whatever sheet was external to the body, a phantom warmth sank. its planar suction [ ] the ~~w~~hole.

poppies. poppies.

california is full of it: gold. the rush
we get from its luster. it drove men
in droves here. the burning sun
cools itself by dipping into the blue,
that's golden, too.
the bridge i see on runs and walks.
your hair, your hair, your hair.
the wicked witch knew its power—i sleep
in the gold of california. the seeds
still stuck in my teeth. a trace
of opiates in the blood. the drive
to dover beach, beyond the exit
for the landfill, the hills beside the freeway
swayed—no—quivered spotty orange.
freckled terracettes. hiking the beach
later that day, i saw more. your face
against the green. your face against
the blue. the currency of home
in a face, yours. the transaction
of memory is an image for its forgotten
name. give me that flower on fire.
give me the word for *unbearable sun.*

Notes and Acknowledgments

A mountain of gratitude to the editors of the magazines who published these poems, a few in alternative iterations: *DIAGRAM*: "a child i don't know asks me what tragedy is." *The Offending Adam*: "hailing clouds," "asperatus" and "late summer." *OmniVerse*: "enantiodromia." *The Cortland Review*: "poppies. poppies." *Eleven Eleven*: "winter poem." *Public Pool*: "weekend." And poems from the sequence entitled "hypnagogia logia" have appeared in both *The Laurel Review* and *Doc Patrick's Journal*.

*

A continent of thanks to the staff at Omnidawn. Rusty Morrison, whose persistently encouraging poetic generosity is a light to walk toward and aspire to.

*

This book is made possible by my partners at speCt! Peter Burghardt, whose misanthropic, cynical, critical nature—for whatever reason—is sieved into motivational insightfulness as it passes through the membrane of our friendship. Gillian Olivia Blythe Hamel, who helped shape this manuscript through her quietly piercing intellect and no-shit editorialship.

*

To the facilitators of and fellow writers at the Saint Mary's MFA program and University Press Books Bookstore community workshops, where many of these poems were conceived and worked on.

*

To all the voices I (un)intentionally hear: Brenda Hillman, Graham Foust, Dora Malech, Shane Book, Matthew Zapruder, David Lau, Cedar Sigo, Geoffrey G. O'Brien, Lyn Hejinian and many others.

*

For my fellow Geminids, my family and friends. For Thayer Giffen, the second weathervane, to whom the title poem and other love poems of this book are dedicated. The future is far away, let's repeat it.

Robert Andrew Perez lives in Berkeley. He is an associate editor for speCt!, a letterpress imprint based out of Oakland, where he also curates readings. He is a recipient of a Lannan prize and a Lambda Literary fellow. Recent work can be found in *The Awl*, *OmniVerse*, *DIAGRAM* and *The Laurel Review*.

The Field
Robert Andrew Perez

Cover art © Job Piston, *David*

Cover and interior text set in Highway Gothic and Gill Sans Std

Cover and interior design by Gillian Olivia Blythe Hamel

Offset printed in the United States
by Edwards Brothers Malloy, Ann Arbor, Michigan
On 55# Glatfelter B18 Antique
Acid Free Archival Quality Recycled Paper

Publication of this book was made possible in part by gifts from:
The New Place Fund
Robin & Curt Caton

Omnidawn Publishing
Oakland, California
2016